Peace Poems
Volume Two

PEACE POEMS
Volume Two

An Anthology
Edited
by
Bethany Reid and Carla Shafer

Published by
Joanne McLain, C.J. Prince, Carol McMillan
and TALA

World Peace Poets

Cover Art: Trish Harding
Front Cover: Bride of Baghdad
Back Cover: Energy From Hell
www.studio-ufo.net

Interior Art: Michael Sturgill

Layout and Design: Joanne McLain

Copyright March 2017

ISBN-13: 978-1544782805
ISBN-10: 1544782802

World Peace Poets
TALA - Teaching and Learning Arts
2308 Lynn Street
Bellingham, WA 98225
chuckanutsandstone.blogspot.com
worldpeacepoets@gmail.com

Introduction

It was a privilege to be asked to co-edit this volume of World Peace Poets. For the most part, the poets hail from the west coast of Washington State and British Columbia, but I am struck by the diversity of locales they bring home to their poems. The local Nooksack River puts in an appearance, and Standing Rock – not too far afield – but also Afghanistan, Viet Nam, Syria, Bangkok, and Dachau. In each poem, no matter its place, I hear the witness of a person who has chosen to dwell in and speak out of his or her particular moment, a moment of political turmoil (a global phenomenon and not isolated to the U.S.), in which war and other acts of violence abound. These poems remind us that peace-making can occur only on the ground on which we stand – even if it looks as though we are merely sitting there, scribbling. Scott Stodola writes, "this life / this life is our only house," and C. J. Prince, in the same vein, reminds us, that we must "go inside [the] heart for peace." Peace is not the opposite of war, as Ashok Bhargava reminds us, and "a single ray of peace is plenty to fire hope / in the dark abyss of [our] desperation." I invite you to read these poems in the spirit in which they were written, not as mere words on pages, but as efforts of peace-making, as declarations of and for peace.

Bethany Reid

Contents

Peace Poems
Volume Two

MᵃˢS 2014

Hometown Hibbing, Minnesota

Elms eaten by army worms cut to stop the spread of disease
stolen pansies excavated and brought home to mother
fireworks celebrate freedom on the Fourth of July
drive-in movies cannot start until the sun is fully set

Stolen pansies excavated and brought home to mother
rust colored water hiding wreckage in emotionless depths
drive-in movies cannot start until the sun is fully set
our village is home to memories of innocence and safety

Rust colored water hiding wreckage in emotionless depths
childhood freedom in fleeting hot summer days
our village is home to memories of innocence and safety
red, white, and blue denim hip huggers on teeny boppers

Childhood freedom in fleeting hot summer days
unending crystal blue skies invite eventual escape
red, white, and blue denim hip huggers on teeny boppers
watermelon eaten outside by children with dripping chins

Unending crystal blue skies invite eventual escape
the nation secured in democracy is safe for today
watermelon eaten outside by children with dripping chins
Seina waters heritage roses in a housedress and slippers

The nation secured in democracy is safe for today
fireworks celebrate freedom on the Fourth of July
Seina waters heritage roses in a housedress and slippers
elms eaten by army worms cut to stop the spread of disease

Sun Coming Out of Cloud Cover

Light on the road
runs toward me, as if lips
of wind might touch me.

I turn as this light plummets,
one green-gold cleft
on the hills.

New Life in Dying Aleppo

The newborn, screaming, red-faced,
held by his feet, upside-down,
slapped, pinched into that first
cry, his first breath angry, the mother
unconscious, gutted on the table, her leg
broken, her arm broken, hauled in 9-months
pregnant, shrapnel in her belly,
the house blown to smithereens around her.
All that death. The baby's
heart silent, the dust, the rubble,
the bombs, almost the last
doctor in ancient Aleppo
saying to a nurse,
"Hand me the scalpel."

action required

absence of conflict
won't by itself bring us peace
cranes are not enough

When Lightning Strikes

When Lightning strikes
from cloud to cloud,
from sky to earth
or earth to sky –
she does all those, you know –
she's negating difference
among her realms.

All life is part electric field
twisting, turning, taking, giving
to and from each other as
we let transients through.
Even in vacuum
all things pass with
electrons and fields caressed.

Beings of the earth and sky
lead different lives,
each charging others
through charges interchanged,
a natural progression
until those differences
become so loaded that
Lightning appears
and throws her spark.
Destruction and conflagration
can result and do.

This is why
both you and I
are charged
to become leaders,
charge-bleeders in our fields

leavening difference
between our heres, their theres.

This is why
both you and I
are charged
to become
lightning rods.

our only house

this life
this life it is our only house
here we close our eyes for night
and for morning and days
have them open
here vitality and competence
are made from infancy and age
see us now
as we are
all with compassion
in this long story
that is also short
this house
this house we want only to live here
only now
only together
our house
outside and inside
together

living always

without voices the dead speak
saying only and always
Honor life
Only the living can listen
Honor life
Only the living can hear
Honor life
Only the living can act
Honor life

And we answer with our lives
through all possible futures
living always and only
within each moment
living always and only
with all consideration
living always and only with all respect
honoring all life
all ways

The Tools of War

One: Giving up on the possibility of peace

Two: Fear of others who can be seen, touched, talked to, known—every separation silences peace like cotton over ear drums

Three: The wheel, where slaves to oil keep it turning, and profiteers ramp up their claims

Four: The voter's pamphlet tossed aside, unread and ballot not delivered

Five: Preventing people from voting because they are black and poor, imprisoned and destitute, undocumented and poor

Six: Belief in white supremacy

Seven: Religious beliefs that push women to the margins, strangle justice with tight hands of doctrine

Eight: Politicians positioning for war, walking away from negotiations

Nine: Children grown for soldiers

Ten: Soldiers at computers viewing people as shadows of heat

Eleven: Soldiers on land, air and sea with their hands holding rifles, and submachine guns

Twelve: Everyone rolling war words off their tongues, like submachine gun, target, collateral damage, good to go

What we know about peace

"Lord, make me an instrument of thy peace."
-St. Francis of Assisi

still tree limb on a quiet day
in the eye of a passing storm
a well-fed hive in winter

the sea on a slack tide
salt air and mud flat spice
floating along the beach

how we sleep, when others do not
resting one's palm on a sleeping partner
a baby's sleep before dreams

a moon shining whole and round
its waning and waxing
repeated for generations

the flock of sheep after morning pasture
any animal fed and resting
undisturbed.

for a time, off the grid,
cell phone silent, no computer
just paper open to your pen

attention to a deeply drawn breath and
its deliberate release—that breath
over and over

silent prayer seeds—young
tendrils of peace
bursting to sprout
amen

May Peace Become Us

Through the sword of history
and the pen of greed,

humanity destroys diversity,
oceans dry up, species starve;

yet come with me to the dance studio,
not to indulge, not even in remorse,

but to return to the ballet barre,
the underbelly that feeds

precision and technique,
until well-practiced in discipline,

through the facts of history,
we realize at home on Earth

that this is the moment
a sentence becomes an outstretched arm and leg,

fingers poised, toes pointed,
eyes focused, head erect,

and in the practice of peace
through grace and beauty, light and music,

the sentence becomes the weight of the world
and the path to Earth's bio-sanctuary:

Honoring and acknowledging Lhaq'temish Traditional
          Territories,
since time immemorial Lhaq'temish,"the People,"
have lived in these territories.

What World, in Our Becoming

What if everything Isaiah and Jesus
and St. John and my mother
said about heaven were only metaphor?
What if the redeemed won't be alone there
or the lion lose its taste for the lamb—
but it was only a way of saying
that heaven is a place of safety?
Maybe heaven's streets aren't paved with gold,
which can't be rugged, anyway, not like cobbles
or macadam, but the ground will be precious to us
as gold was to ancient kings.
Will it be day and "no more night,"
or only so stunningly different from what we know now
that a figure of speech for "indescribable"
is the only way to describe it?
In the womb the infant becomes itself,
forming nose and eye, tongue and ear,
all estranged from need
in its cramped world of salt water,
products of the body's longing for air and light.
How cramped is this world compared to the next?
When the Apostle Paul said,
"Now I see as through a glass darkly,"
what if he wasn't using a metaphor
but making a promise of clarity to come?
What do we long for, not only great shampoo
and excellent deodorant, the perfect beer,
but maybe compassion, maybe peace,
and plenty. What would these look like—
one hand in another? Jars of tomatoes
arranged on a shelf? A sword
beaten into a plowshare? What world,
in our becoming, do we now create?

Immensity

"All angels are terrible" -Rilke

and they might be angels,
the immensity of their bodies
moving through nights drenched

in moonlight,
like horses crossing a snowfield,
bodies of silver

not clanking but moving soundless,
breathless, the weight
of their hooves a vibration

we feel first in our soles
and then in our souls,
a dull thudding,

a heart beating under a hand,
a clapperless bell ringing—

The Search

When you look for universes
beyond Orion's belt,
when you traipse after leprechauns
and only find an empty meadow
with no rainbow, no pot of gold,
when you force magic,
You cannot see it.

Go inside your heart for peace.
For peace is magic, not legerdemain
nor incantations. Just that last twinkle
of twilight through cedar and maple.
The moment that suspends all,
there but for a breath.
There is peace.

Chaos to Tranquility

She falls through the crack,
Like Alice or Mrs. Tittlemouse.
Red polka-dot heels fly away.
No up or down.
Vertigo spins headlines
in a psychedelic faerie tale.
She will cast her vote
like dropping a faceted ruby
In the river Styx
and pray for peace.

Classified Ad: Seeking Peace?

Drop in class to gain inner peace.
Bring one impatiens of a thousand
species. Modify your intake
of moonlight. Drink
42 drops of dragon milk.
No pre-registration required.
Random unpredictable results.

Whose Curtain?

Curtain fences thick
Embroidered red silk keeps US in.
Purple dragons dance one on top of the other.

Keep we monkeys in the good life.
Millions of starving children and deceased
civilians? Truth hides in in polka dotted mud.

Witches and Warlocks stay clean
Walk through the oil spill of politics.
Monkeys stay covered in slime.
Bombs reinforce super power.
Visitors venture into forests made opium happy.
Confused images kept loose and flappy.

Wind blows shield open.
Music's played and monkeys dance.
Doctors blown to bits.

Dorothys fell into magic kingdom.
Multi Corporate Minds add fancy words.
Explorers kept stoned and happy.

Dorothys' dreams cause her to face
Water Protectors AND Monied class of secrets.
Struggles add to conflicts.

Disguises keep light rays away.
Monkeys fear power so attack Dorothys.
Dorothys' team brings brains, heart, courage.

Flames surround all.
Water on fire,

18

Witches and Warlocks attack.

Good Green witch works for peaceful strength,
Whisking her sharing wand.
Dorothys and She travel to Standing Rock.

Once warring tribes and neighbors new and old
Stand together for Water is Life.
Some workers and veteran heroes follow.

Peace prayers keep Dorothys strong.
Keep Standing Rock's Peaceful Example.

What Price For Peace

"…lemons for sale, five cents each or, three for a dime"
I hear there is an auction for peace today.
    A rich merchant is going to sell it to the highest bidder.
    I wonder what the going price will be.
    What kind of peace is it?
Maybe—peace in the world
              Will the price be 10 billion lives
              Or, a simple agreement?
              Destruction of the earth
              Or, a simple humane compromise?
I can only guess
Maybe—peace of mind
Will the price be blindness to reality
              Or, seeing all and trying?
              Becoming deaf and mute
              Or, know the truth and speaking the truth
                  Not backing down?
I can only guess
Maybe—peace with others
    Will the price be selling your soul to be on top
    Or, living down here, making the best of it?
    Putting love in a communicable disease ward
Or, spreading it around?
Becoming an island and a hermit
Or, building bridges and mingling?

I can only guess and maybe hope.

20

Battle

Tightly structured
words turn inward.

Fear holds
tighter than promises.

Afterwards walls of silence,
of denial, evidence of the past,

heaped in piles, a rubble of
vapid sentences lying about us.

Oneifbylandtwoifbysea. Mantras,
catechisms, obligations, certainties,

determinisms, the casual observer
mute, the sage dismembered

by his own predilection of drafting
patriotic verses, lauding the pursuit

of manifist destiny. Number
one on the hit parade. A sky

no longer yielding its flight of birds.

Catch phrases scream in a night,
more intense than the rockets

red glare, demanding obedience,
proclaiming victory. Ignoring

the wounded who walk
among us.

White Angel (*)

Hope sparks
action in the angry men
gathering in breadlines,
their wives and children

hungry, sick, filled
with desperation.
A grizzled man,
holds an empty cup,

rests his weary arms
atop a withered railing.
Unshaven, he turns away
his gnarled hands folded,

eyes hidden, portals he does
not wish to share with others.

Only the shuttered moment
gives pain instant immortality.

> (*) Written in response to a Dorothea Lange
> photograph of the White Angel Bread Line, San
> Francisco, 1932.

Fleeing to Standing Rock, Riding on Magic -
December 7, 2016

Fleeing unimagined results of a
presidential election.
Fleeing unintentional ignorance of
White privilege.
Anger and chaos
narrowed and focused,
honed to a
laser of intent:
I fled to Standing Rock.

Friends came to load my car.
Lora joined me as navigator.
Thunder Hinmato'oyalahq'it
Met us on the road with
Lanterns, axes, and a giant gas heater.
In Spokane there were
mountaineering tents,
down bags and jackets.
Impossibly, my SUV,
"Cinnamon's", cargo space
expanded with magic
till everything offered fit in.
My war pony bulged with
Supplies and with prayers.

Nearing Bozeman
In winter night
Black ice
Black night
Red truck tail lights far ahead.
Hold her steady

Tap the brakes
Barely a touch
Without effect.
Ride it out
No curves
Infinite time
Infinite road
Infinite blackness up ahead.
Less glare?
Grey road?
Feel a grip.
Barely.
Touch again
Slowing
Fifty to forty
Yes.
Thirty
Control.

December first dawn
turned snowy plains pink.
Today we would reach Standing Rock.
We'd heard of the road blocks,
$1,000 fines
for those with supplies.
Taking back roads,
We found our way clear.
On a bumpy dirt road,
cleared of yesterday's blizzard,
we rolled into camp.

"We have salmon and cedar
and heaters for camp,"
I said to the keepers of the gate.
With welcoming smiles
They told us where to find

Dan Nanamkin's and Rosebud's camps
in the maze of tipis, yurts, and tents
sprawled along the river's floodplain.
Past the sacred fire,
we found our friends.
We were greeted with hugs and
joy at the chocolate bars,
fleece vests,
dried jerky and fruit,
tampons and hand warmers,
dollars and hats.
Dan took the boxes.
Jason brought a sled;
he'd deliver the rest.

We prayed at the fire
then walked up the hill
for a final delivery:
the song I must sing.
A Northern Cheyenne song
had been taught me by Sheila,
my sister and friend.
In a voice not my own
in a language not mine,
the song for the warriors
came out loud and strong,
to cover the camp.
"Young man, when you go into battle,
Don't look back.
Keep your eyes forward.
We are behind you.
Our prayers
Our strength
Our love."
Lora joined in
the repeated refrain.

With tears on our cheeks
we finished the song.
A young man appeared,
taking my arm,
helping me over the ice,
back down to our car.

Riding on magic
We headed back home.
A delivery only
of supplies and a song.
In another reality,
protected by spirits,
we traveled in joy.
Seven days we drove.
Two thousand seven hundred and
forty-four miles.
The journey a privilege.

On our last day
the announcement came:
Dakota Access Pipeline's
easement across sacred
Sioux land was denied.
The Water Protectors
had won their first battle.
With courage, with peace,
and with wisdom as rifles,
they still continue the war.

This is a House of Peace

Come in here, come in.
The table is spread for you,
awaiting your presence.
This is a House of Peace.
Now the signals rise from the hills,
sounding loud into the valleys of hope:
Peace has come.
We are here, together,
in the moment of realization,
we are one.

This is a House of Peace.
Come in and join us
around the table,
feel the warmth of the fire within
as we speak together of the future.
This is a House of Peace.

Beyond Unfriending

I have a hard time with the arguments.
Enraged through and through,
heart racing
disgusted and shocked
when my own family (chosen or born into)
cannot grasp the
blunt and obvious horror
of another life cut short
      on the street
      opening the door
      lying down
      taking a drive with the family.
The omnipresent videos
defying the skewed and oppressive
lessons of Whiteness
(to which I too was not immune:
"Bad Apples" and "No Other Choice").
Truth to decipher ourselves.
Evidence beyond
the pushed aside stories of hundreds of years.
The standard of evidence Whiteness has insisted upon,
Denied.

Nearly everyday
you are given hard proof that
compliance and tone
are irrelevant.
That police reports can be manipulated or purely invented.
All is there for you to compare, side by side,
further corroborated by
testimonies of loved ones and survivors,
from mothers, teachers, the president, and my god
even police officers themselves—

"Not enough!"

Hundreds, thousands in the streets,
Arrested, molested, threatened, gassed
RISKING
jobs, health, life itself.
"MLK would never!" you respond,
"If only they asked politely"
as if this had never been tried.

So today I write this poem.
An exploratory mission
to find the secret strings of your heart,
the ones beyond
logic and fear
that can resonate with a clarity
my furious internet arguments can't.

I offer this to you,
that you may come to understand
some
of the love, rage and broken-heartedness
of grieving communities
beyond your own,
beyond this poem,
beyond the power and privilege to ignore,

that the ease with which you tell me
"They must have deserved it"
is forever disturbed,

That you may one day say, "No more!"

The change being grown around you
is sown with love and moral rage,
the necessary nutritive facts to create peace

for all,
even you,
whether or not you choose to step out
of the false comfort of your disbelief.

On the Horizon a Field of Grass, No Visible Scars of War

A soldier's request.
Anoint my body with blood
from a lineage of warriors.
Absolution and resilience;
I pledge my life.
Send me out to the battle beaten plain,
soil churned by tank track,
> calvary hoof,
> legion foot.

I am commanded to defend
a way of living:
> coffee on every street-corner,
> money from machines in stone walls,
> heat at the touch of a button,
> light at the flip of a switch,
> food in packages with "sell-by" dates.

Allow me to earn my salt in joyful obligation,
> defending words in a breath,
> print on a page,
> worship of a chosen god,
> love and more love.

Rain, anoint me.
For peace, I will sacrifice my wind blessed body.

The Water Will Flow Clean

black snake coils to strike, to slither south, never receding
they come on foot, in cars, in trucks, all yellowed and dusty
woman with a fae name feeds 3000 campers three times a day
they wear worn jeans and t-shirts, NO DAPL lettered red

they come on foot, in cars, in trucks, all yellowed and dusty
peace is a carved totem pole blessed by many hands
they wear worn jeans and t-shirts, NO DAPL lettered red
peace is a Scotsman at Dachau telling of Standing Rock

peace is a carved totem pole blessed by many hands
man whose name means gladness hugs the backhoe tight
peace is a Scotsman at Dachau telling of Standing Rock
prayers lift skyward on voices and feet drum the soil

man whose name means gladness hugs the backhoe tight
they wear buckskin, fringed, beaded with stars, feathered
prayers lift skyward on voices and feet drum the soil
they bear drums, pipes, blankets, flags, young children

they wear buckskin, fringed, beaded with stars, feathered
peace is the voice of a youngster wise in the ways of justice
they bear drums, pipes, blankets, flags, young children
peace is the gathering of hearts and hands for clean water

peace is the voice of a youngster wise in the ways of justice
woman with a fae name feeds 3000 campers three times a day
peace is the gathering of hearts and hands for clean water
black snake coils to strike, to slither south, never receding

Trespassing

So ancient is attributing a difficult
common past with borders which have moved with
        conquest.
North and South share varieties which differ only
        regionally.
Garbures and melted cheese have a common
heritage left by domination, the trade of crops exposed
by the wake of Christopher Columbus and his single
revolutionary event.

"Native" means merely "before there" to the question
"What is Native?" "What is imported?"
No inconsiderable number of cursory tales
reveal how and when importation occurred
over many routes, circled the globe East
to West, like germs widespread, before
the arrival of "civilization" and "culture."
A specific case: coastal towns feared raids long before
        white feet,
conflicts with pirates imbue the legends

Conquest, persuasive and pervasive in its instruction,
charts its own course
landscaping generations.

Composed of redactions from text found in The Old World Kitchen
by Elizabeth Luard and Filipino Folktales *by Dean Fansler.*

Silence War/Sing Peace

I hope your bombs' exploding roars
and rifle snipers' zings
are silenced soon
by rays of happy words,
so mothers crooning babies to sleep
in local homes can be heard after
the cheering songs of Peacemakers.

As we now clap in this pouring rain
after a Sahara dry summer
of browning scenery
with only roaring forest fires
with fierce, multi-metre high flames
devouring homes, farms,
orchards and many wild animals,
even gulping fire fighters,
searing flesh to ash.

We cheer for rains of hope
for you and yours in war battle
sites and sounds around the globe
returning home alive
to your loved ones
so you too can sing Peace.

"Small Acts", Black Moss Press, Canada Fall 2016

Peace Holiday

Just a clean surface
on everything and everyone
to be noticed and absorbed
as the first time -

be curious again
thrillingly open to all,
just an hourglass focus of stillness
memory locking wonder,
entering moonrise or waterfall
by choice,
feeling your heart warming
or weeping, truly awake
to living.

"Imagining Lives", Black Moss Press, 2012

Homage to the West Side

Go! Go!
Go man!
Go, you son of a lamppost gang!
Go, man,
follow,
Footsteps pacing on before.
Keep step!
Don't stop!

Hair swept up in latest custom,
fingers clenching deep in pocket,
round the smooth hard ebon handle
of a real cool switchblade knife.
Joined now with the hood's elite,
plunging headlong down the street,
errant knights on quest uncertain,
rendezvous with death or life!

Go, go man, go!
Fix your face with mask of stoic!
Go, man.
 Show it,
at thirteen you can make your mark.
No time to think,
Not time to shrink!
Not now!

Your brother Dominick's stiff body
lies in state in cold-lit morgue.
Like a mantle wear Dom's jacket,
pocket weighted with his gun.
Feel its pendulum's swing motion,
as the battle's fast approaching,

push on through your fate's dark curtain,
pounding pavement, pulsing, run.

Go!
Go, man,
Go, novitiate of blood.
Don't slow,
rite of passage is at hand.
Battle's nigh;
someone will die.
Just go!

Footsteps from the dawns of story
echo down from tree-lined trails.
Young men bearing dreams of glory
from oft-repeated old men's tales,
balance them 'gainst fear of dying
by the hand of despised foe,
lying words of glory, lying,
can not make all fear to go.

There's a fear far worse than dying
outcast days, love, honor lost.
lying words of war's great glory,
lying words of cowards' cost.

Feel the ancient call and go now.
There is nothing else to know now.
Old men lying,
Young men dying,
Mothers crying,
go, go,
go child,
go!

A World in Your Eyes

Irresistible cravings
lead us to supernatural realms,
Call us to places of peace and beauty.

Transcend to lakes of blue, captivate,
enchant the soul.
Carry us to this sacred oasis where
sand crystals from time's hourglass
flow eternally free.

Where valleys of fire burn
their beauty onto the mind's eye,
vermillion cliffs haunt our dreams,
tantalize our senses.

Nature appeals to the seductive
as she cast's her mystical spell.
Follow me, rise with the trees
to touch the glad sky,
We can do nothing more.
In sweet surrender we soar—
Our love on high.

Take my hand,
we need not travel far
to our memory dream land.

All is in sight within each other's eyes.

Caught Distraught
~written while sitting on a hillside looking over the Mekong River

Lightning in the distance,
a shot in purest black;
caused by a disturbance
to keep opponents back.

Caught distraught in silence
upon a darkened hill;
why all of this nonsense,
this civic urge to kill?

Frantic at the outrage
of people gone deranged;
confine them in a cage
so peace can be arranged!

Personally speaking,
I'm tired of all the hate!
Can't we start uniting
before it's just too late?

Here I sit in safety
merely thinking of the past.
How much longer will it be,
until we're dead at last?

How can our leaders
agree on any plan
to become the hunters
and cause the death of MAN?

On Observing a Vietnam Vet

He's been through more in just a couple years
a long-ish time ago than you or I
just average folk can even comprehend
when looking in the back parts of our minds
we'd rather forget, or say we couldn't find.
Just watching him you see he left some things
there, lying under trees—what youth he had,
what self-assuredness, feeling of pride,
and sense of dignity he might have clung to.
And hear him speak—it's clear not all the world
is right yet: if it were, he wouldn't bear
the weight of it in words. It seems that if
he laughed it still would have the pall of death.

We didn't ask him to carry the weight of the world
on his shoulders. We just gave him no choice.

This Stillness
Waking up after returning from Bangkok

I want to be strung here perpetually
Just you and the great quiet ocean and me
And the frost on the trees and the mist in the air
We're waking up here—yesterday, we were there!

Between ending one journey and starting another
We're floating in stillness, and I'm starting to wonder
How all of this stillness can possibly be
When in front and behind there's a veritable stream
Of commotion and chaos and salt and red dust,
And the shuffling of pages, and I think that I must be
Imagining this! How it rings in my ears!
The frost in the yard, the space between years.

It's an infinite space, that spectacular span,
Between years, between journeys, between "could..."
        and "CAN",
Between waiting for something and making it true
And though there are—both there AND here
        —things to do,
this feeling of stillness is unusual, and new...
I'd like to stay here, in the stillness, with you.

Breathe In Sound—Release Silence

stop
sit
close your eyes, breathe in

open your mind, breathe out
listen for reconciliations
accept each—boundless

clouds crash—countries collide
winds whistle—whip
like melody's strength of strings

squeal of young children
screech of gulls
harmony's screaming song

breathe in sound
open your eyes
get up

go
stand up
release silence

To Peace from Our Dis-ease

In dream I search for you,
a holy silence that was once here
in this place of multiplicity.

I try to sort, accumulate your inference,
attach it to my stockpile of imaginings
that braid three thousand reminiscences

of better times. As if accumulating
memories like sand and stones
might save us all before we scatter

into vacant lots. But still you sit
beside me, on this soiled verge,
content to slip though gutter's grate.

We grow restless when we can't commit.
We fight, fly headlong into hapless mime,
our hooded sweatshirts working overtime.

Dark flitters where I looked for you
and lost your daylight common sense
though you reached to touch my face.

I know you have chosen to return,
as a stillness we may recognize,
and free us, after all we have to hide.

On Her Way to Standing Rock

I am old,
she says, though
she's still full of flame,
got some battles left in her
or she wouldn't be following
her heart all the way
to North Dakota.

I'll stay in motels
not drive straight through
like I used to do,
take three days going
maybe two coming back,
depends on what I find.

Into her car she's stuffed
plastic bins with fleece vests
bought out at the Goodwill,
blankets, sleeping bags,
a case of Honey Crisp apples,
some Swiss chocolate.
Her jacket pocket droops
with dollars donated
from friends fueled
by her fervor.

We have a forever hug
and I memorize the curves
of her body thinking
we must both feel like bears
to each other,
round and soft bundled
in layers of wool and down,

44

warm to the bone,
unlike the Water Protectors
shivering in Deep North
snow, though when we part
her smile is sun stabbing
through storm clouds,
radiating hope.

.

Exercising for Change

My son does push-ups for the dead,
twenty-two each day
for men and women,
U. S. veterans
who end their lives
by their own hands
nearly one
every
hour.

He brings attention
to this staggering statistic,
to its epidemic cause
unresolved
Post **T**raumatic **S**tress **D**isorder,
by videotaping himself,
asking others
to do the same
in a spirit of compassion,
non-violence,
peace,
and they are.

What was at first a painful
slow struggle
has built momentum,
and now my son's body
and those of others
are fast-pumping
levers of hope,
one plus one plus one person
working
to make a difference.

Peace Rocks

On the shores of the Nooksack
we choose volcanic stones
and place them in large fires
in preparation for our sweat lodge
on the ancient, sacred land.

These special rocks are called stone people.
They live in peace.
Stones...Rock...Peace.

The lodge is cinched up tight.
Inside men and women pray
and talk with the stones
which twinkle under offerings of sweetgrass.
Sometimes I see blue lights.

The stones sweat and the people
get hotter and hotter.
They sweat out their prayers, drum and sing
for family, clan and nation.

Daylight hours pass,
the night wears on
bringing peace
in the womb of the lodge.

At last our voices are quiet,
silent with heartfelt reflections.
How long can we sit still
in graceful balance
with the rocks, the breathing land
and the reality of peace?

Illegal Aliens / Refugees

They will keep pouring in like sand grains
in an hourglass and slip through the fingers.

They will blow over like dust storm
if we build walls to stop them.

Shiploads of humanity will continue to cry
out loud before every sunrise on our shores.

Even if we don't want them to show up
and where else could they go.

Syria, Iraq or Afghanistan: simply burn them to ashes
in the name of light.

Just a single ray of peace is plenty to fire hope
in the dark abyss of their desperation.

We can light peace
if we really want to.

ASHOK BHARGAVA, a prolific poet, an inspiring writer, and a committed community activist. Writing in English and Hindi, he has published several collections of his poems: *Mirror of Dreams, A Kernel of Truth,* and *Lost in the Morning Calm,* among others. (Vancouver, BC)

ELIZABETH CARARELLI holds strong personal/spiritual development values and green, socially responsible ideals that she uses to empower her writing as a healing tool for humanity and to awaken consciousness globally. (Bellingham, WA)

SUSAN CHASE-FOSTER travels the world. Her poems and stories have appeared in *Clover, Noisy Water, Memory into Memoir, Whatcom Writes!* anthologies and *Cirque.* She's a two-time winner of the Sue C. Boynton Poetry contest, and is currently at work on a book of poems and photos from Taipei. (Bellingham, WA)

LINDA CONROY is co-host of Bellingham's Village Books poetry group and a Sue Boynton Poetry Contest winner. She believes that poetry informs and foreshadows, and serves well to honor the complexity and simplicity of human nature. (Bellingham, WA)

JOHN S GREEN believes in the peaceful power of words over war, and the budget is certainly more reasonable for what you get in return. (Bellingham, WA)

EVAN INGALLS, composer, teacher, and musician was born and raised in Bellingham. He studied Music Composition and Linguistics at WWU, and works with Bellingham Arts Academy for Youth and the Whatcom Hills Waldorf School. He writes poetry to process his world.

KARL KING Writing since 1971 Karl has published in *Grunt Mag, Free Spirit Journal, The Connection, The Woods-Runner, The Nocturnal Lyric,* and *Writing.com.* Karl focuses on non-violence, anti-NWO and love themes. He posts positive-themed haiku on Facebook and reads at various Bellingham venues.

JANET KVAMMEN, Vice-President of the Royal City Literary Arts Society, is an award-winning poet, artist, and photographer. Janet is active on the local poetry & arts scene. Her work has been published in numerous poetry anthologies. (New Westminster, BC)

VINCE LANDI works in different genres: poems, essays, stories and plays. Many of his writings protest dehumanizing forces that beset us. Besides frequent readings at Open Mics, his pieces have been published in *Clover*, and *The Whatcom Watch*; and also have been produced on KMRE's Community Playhouse. (Bellingham, WA)

BERNICE LEVER, in 10th poetry book, Small Acts - 2016, shares her Motto: 'Common acceptance can flourish to true compassion, then loving actions lead to PEACE.' From her Bowen Island, BC, Canada home, she delves deep into romance, politics, eco-disasters and nature's gifts. www.colourofwords.com

REBECCA MABANGLO MAYOR received her MFA in Creative Writing from Pacific Lutheran University in 2012. Her thesis *Pele's Fire* centered on themes of loss and reclamation in terms of identity, community, and heritage. Her poetry chapbook *Pause Mid-Flight* was released in 2010. Her poetry, fiction, and memoir have appeared in several anthologies.

KATHLEEN MCKEEVER, a teacher of esoteric skills, uses tarot and her nature based spiritual practice as inspiration for her healing rituals and poetry. The labyrinth in her back yard serves as anchor and portal. Bellingham, WA Lummi/Nooksack Territories.

TINA MCKIM – Cheese eater, rabble rouser, thing maker, disabled and totally awesome. (Bellingham, WA)

JOANNE MCLAIN, PH.D., is the coauthor of *Catching My Breath*. She can be found walking and observing the world from her home in Parker, Colorado.

CAROL MCMILLAN, PH.D., has several academic publications. Her poetry and memoirs have been published in several anthologies, and she is the author of one book, *White Water, Red Walls*, chronicling in poetry, photographs, and paintings her rafting trip down the Grand Canyon. She is a recipient of the Sue C. Boynton Poetry Merit Award. (Bellingham, WA)

JIM MILSTEAD, a member of Independent Writers Studio, demonstrated against the Vietnam war. He has been attending the Bellingham Peace Vigil since 9/11. His adroit and skillful writing and his spirit for community inspires all writers. (Bellingham, WA)

DOBBIE REESE NORRIS, Wordsworth curator for the Health & Culture Committee of the City of Seattle, founding member of Floating Mountain Poets, a performing troupe and featured in May, 2005 *Las Cruces Poets and Writers Magazine*, he founded Seattle's Third Tuesdays Poets & Writers. He is a member of poetrynight & Whatcom Poetry Series. (Bellingham, WA)

BARBARA CEIS PERRY, A third generation Washingtonian, has played as a child in a freshly cut old growth forest, driven on the newly opened I-5 freeway, traveled, returned home to raise a family, marched in many peace vigils, and taught at local tribal nations. (Bellingham, WA)

C.J. PRINCE was Another Mother for Peace in the 1960s. Now she is Another Great Grandmother for Peace who persists and resists with words. Her poetry book *Mother, May I?* is available on Amazon. She is a co-founder of World Peace Poets. (Bellingham, WA)

BETHANY REID grew up in southwest Washington on a farm nestled in the Willapa hills. Her most recent book of poems, *Sparrow*, won the 2012 Gell Poetry Prize, selected by Dorianne Laux. Her blog is, www.awritersalchemy.wordpress.com She lives in Edmonds, WA with her husband and daughters.

BETTY SCOTT'S writing adventures as a poet and essayist began when she was employed at *The Wenatchee World*. Her collection *Central Heating*, poems of love and loss in celebration of living on planet earth, will be published in early summer of 2017 by Cave Moon Press (Bellingham, WA)

CARLA SHAFER, founder of Chuckanut Sandstone Writers Theater, has poems published in *Connections, Whatcom Places II* and her chapbook *Remembering the Path*. She has been named an International Poetry Ambassador by Writers International Network of Canada and the West Coast Tagore Society. (Bellingham, WA)

SCOTT STODOLA has been a student and a teacher in three states, two countries and one of the Pacific Islands. He has three grown children, is learning how to blow a bugle with his grandchildren and is still puzzling over how people learn to live with each other in equanimity.

GARY WADE, an Iowan by birth and Washingtonian by choice, his poetry has been published in *Clover, A Literary Rag* and several printed anthologies and chapbooks. Awards include a Sue C. Boynton Walk Award and a Pushcart nomination. Gary believes poets should occasionally stand as social critics and philosophers.

F.E. WALLS loves traveling and living in places as diverse as Wales and Botswana. Her poems appear in *Pontoon, Ekphrasis, damselfly press, Avocet, Strange Poetry* among others as well as the anthology, *Writing Across Cultures*. (Seattle, WA)

RICHARD WIDERKEHR's new book, *In The Presence Of Absence*, will be published in Fall, 2017, by MoonPath Press. His other books: are *The Way Home* (Plain View Press) and *Her Story of Fire* (Egress Studio Press). He's had poems in *Cirque* and *Rattle*; others will be in *Measure, Jeopardy*, and *Arts & Letters*.

J.L. WRIGHT is a fulltime RVer enjoying learning about the great northwest by exploring the Bellingham area for an extended stay. J. L. wishes to start conversations about current issues through a poetic voice.

MS 2014

62063813R00037

Made in the USA
Lexington, KY
28 March 2017